Alan Bern

KLEZMER

14 MITTELSCHWERE STÜCKE FÜR **AKKORDEON M2**

14 INTERMEDIATE-LEVEL PIECES FOR **ACCORDION**

Inhalt • Contents • Table des matières

Alan Bern: Klezmer Accordion

Cover design by drevseiterweiter
Photo of Alan Bern: © David Kaufman, 2010

UE 36 122
ISMN 979-0-008-08587-1
UPC 8-03452-06968-3
ISBN 978-3-7024-7256-6

Vorwort

Die Stücke in diesem Band sind Bearbeitungen bekannter und weniger bekannter jiddischer Instrumentalmelodien für solo Standardbass-Akkordeon. Sie repräsentieren verschiedene Genres, die für die Klezmer-Musik des 19. bis 21. Jahrhunderts typisch sind. Der Band ist für Akkordeon-Spieler der Mittelstufe konzipiert, und die Stücke werden fortlaufend anspruchsvoller. Der Schüler lernt, technische Schwierigkeiten im Bass und Melodiebereich des Instrumentes zu meistern.

Viele Melodien des Klezmer-Repertoires finden sich auch in der griechischen, türkischen, rumänischen und in anderen Musiktraditionen. Der distinktiv jiddische Stil entsteht durch die Art und Weise, in welcher ein Klezmer-Musiker eine Melodie phrasiert und verziert. Diese Nuancen sind jedoch im Notenbild nicht erkennbar – jeder Musiker muss zunächst durch viel Zuhören ein Gefühl für die Musik entwickeln, das er dann auf seine Interpretation der Stücke übertragen kann. Ich empfehle Ihnen, möglichst viele verschiedene Aufnahmen der Stücke in diesem Band anzuhören, insbesondere solche aus den ersten Jahrzehnten des 20. Jahrhunderts, da in dieser Zeit der Stil mit all seinen Nuancen noch intakt war. Zusätzlich sollten Sie die Online-Einführung zu diesem Band unter www.universaledition.com/klezmer-accordion-extra herunterladen. Darin werden Themen wie *Klezmer-Musik – Gestern und heute*, *Das Akkordeon in der Klezmer-Musik* oder *Harmonik* behandelt.

Bevor Sie sich ganz der Musik dieses Bandes widmen, sollten Sie die Hinweise zu Phrasierung, Verzierung und der Bassnotation in *Anhang 1* lesen. *Anhang 2* ergänzt dies mit einer kurzen Beschreibung zu jedem Stück.

Ich habe diese Stücke ausgewählt, weil sie mir am Herzen liegen und ich finde, dass sie mit den Jahren an Schönheit gewinnen. Ich hoffe, dass sie Ihnen genauso viel Freude bereiten werden wie mir.

Alan Bern, Dezember 2013

Preface

The pieces in this collection are arrangements for solo, standard-bass accordion of some well-known and some less-well-known Yiddish instrumental melodies. They represent several different genres common in klezmer music of the 19th to the 21st centuries. Although intended for the 'intermediate-level' accordionist, the music increases in technical difficulty throughout the book. The pieces pose different technical challenges for both the bass and melody sides of the instrument.

Many melodies in the klezmer repertoire also exist in Greek, Turkish, Romanian and other musical traditions. The way a klezmer musician phrases and ornaments a melody gives it its distinctively Yiddish flavor. But such nuances are not evident in the notation itself; each musician has to gain an aural understanding of the style from many hours of listening and bring that understanding to the written notes. I strongly recommend supplementing this book with listening to as many recordings of each piece as possible, preferably from the early decades of the 20th century, when the nuances of style were still intact. I equally recommend downloading the online introduction to this book available at: www.universaledition.com/klezmer-accordion-extra. It covers topics such as *Klezmer music, then and now, The accordion in klezmer music, Harmony* and more.

Before diving into the music, please see *Appendix 1* for an essential guide to phrasing, ornamentation and the bass notation system used in this book. *Appendix 2* provides brief information about each individual piece.

I chose these pieces because I love them and find that their beauty only grows greater over time. I hope that they will give you as much pleasure as they have given me.

Alan Bern, December 2013

Préface

Vous trouverez dans ce recueil des arrangements pour accordéon chromatique solo de mélodies instrumentales yiddish, certaines connues, d'autres moins. Ils représentent plusieurs genres différents répandus dans la musique klezmer du XIXe au XXIe siècle. Bien que destinées aux accordéonistes d'un niveau « intermédiaire », les pièces augmentent en difficulté technique au fil du recueil. Elles offrent donc plusieurs défis techniques à surmonter, à la main gauche comme à la main droite.

Beaucoup d'airs du répertoire klezmer existent aussi dans la musique populaire grecque, turque, roumaine etc. Ce sont le phrasé et les ornements apportés par le musicien qui donnent à la mélodie son caractère typiquement yiddish. Mais ces nuances ne sont pas évidentes dans la notation ; il faut écouter et encore écouter pour se mettre le style « dans l'oreille », puis utiliser cette expérience pour interpréter la partition. En complément à ce recueil, je recommande vivement d'écouter autant d'enregistrements que possible de chaque pièce, datant de préférence des premières décennies du XXe siècle, alors que les nuances du style étaient encore vivaces. Je vous invite aussi à télécharger l'introduction au recueil, disponible ici : www.universaledition.com/klezmer-accordion-extra. Elle vous en apprendra plus sur *La musique klezmer d'hier à aujourd'hui*, *L'accordéon dans la musique klezmer*, *L'harmonie* etc.

Avant de vous plonger dans la musique, lisez l'*annexe 1*, pour des explications essentielles sur le phrasé, l'ornementation et le système de notation des basses utilisé dans ce recueil. L'*annexe 2* donne une petite description de chaque morceau.

J'ai choisi des pièces que j'aime, des pièces qui ne font que gagner en beauté avec le temps, et j'espère que vous aurez autant de plaisir que moi à les jouer.

Alan Bern, decembre 2013

D-freygish Hora

Traditional
arr. Alan Bern

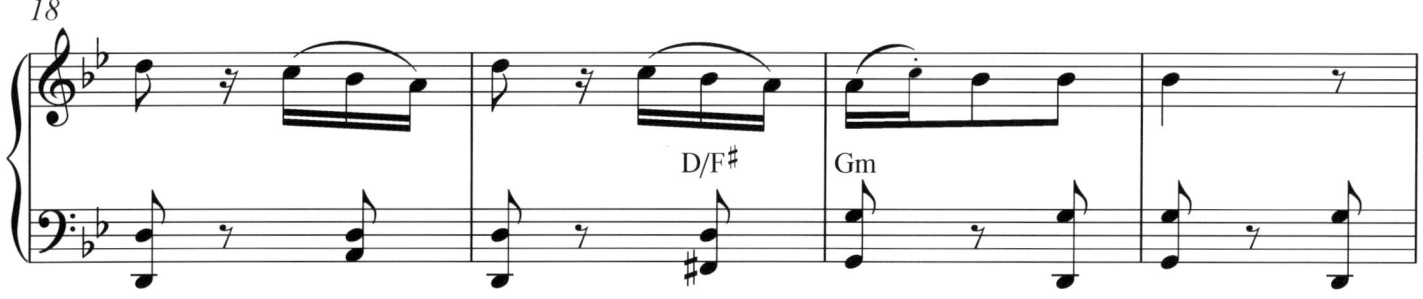

Universal Edition UE 36 122

Kandel's Hora

Traditional
arr. Alan Bern

UE 36 122

Moldavian Yiddish Hora

Traditional
arr. Alan Bern

Beachten Sie bitte, dass in diesem Stück d im Basssystem immer eine Bassnote ist und kein Akkord.
Note: In this piece, the D on the middle line of the bass staff is always a bass note, not a chord.
Note : dans cette pièce, le *ré* sur la ligne médiane de la portée de basse est toujours une note de basse, non un accord.

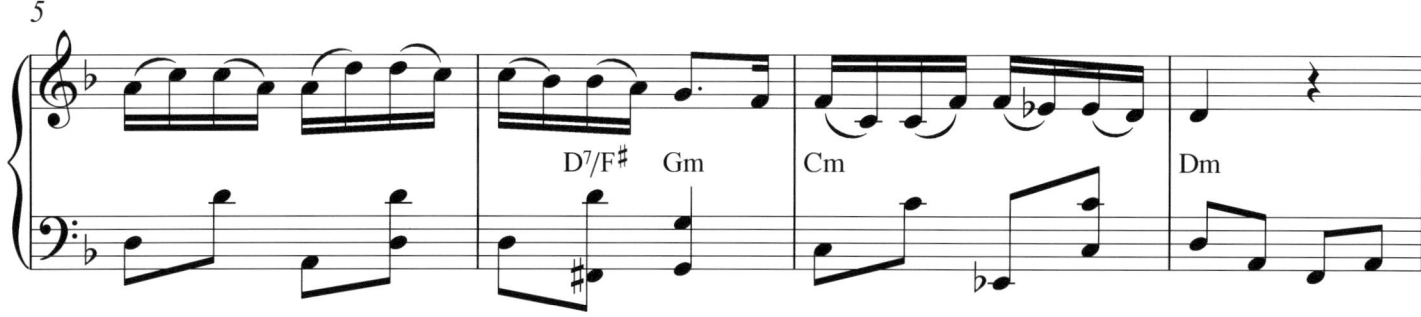

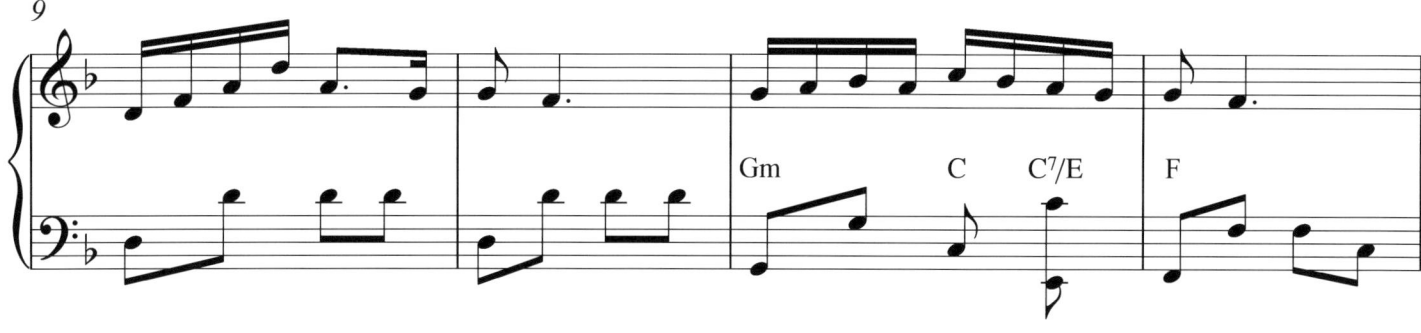

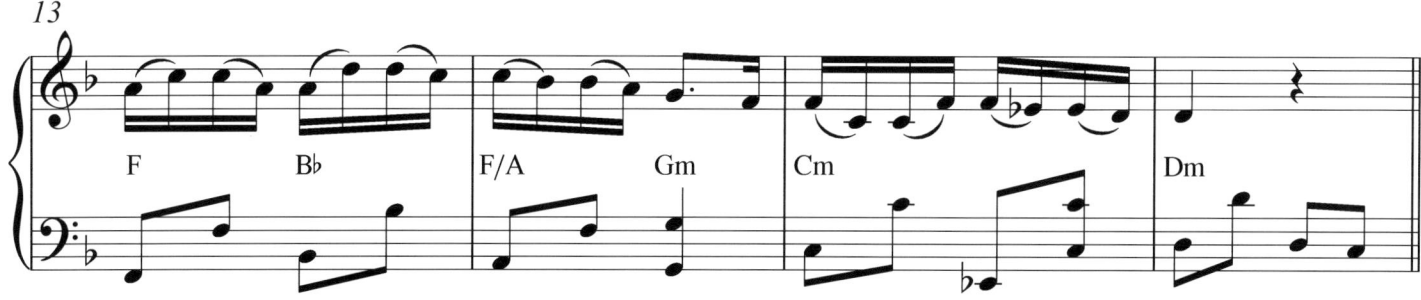

UE 36 122

Moldavian Yiddish Suite

Traditional
arr. Alan Bern

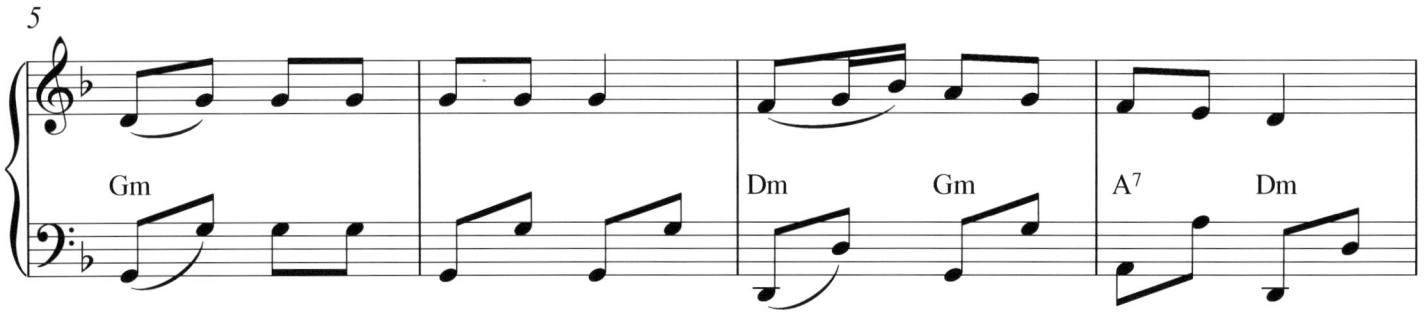

UE 36 122

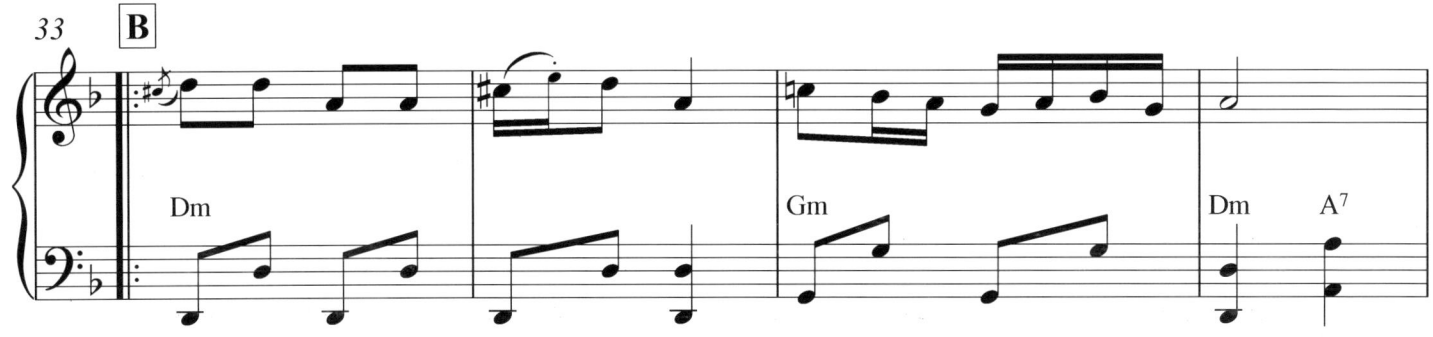

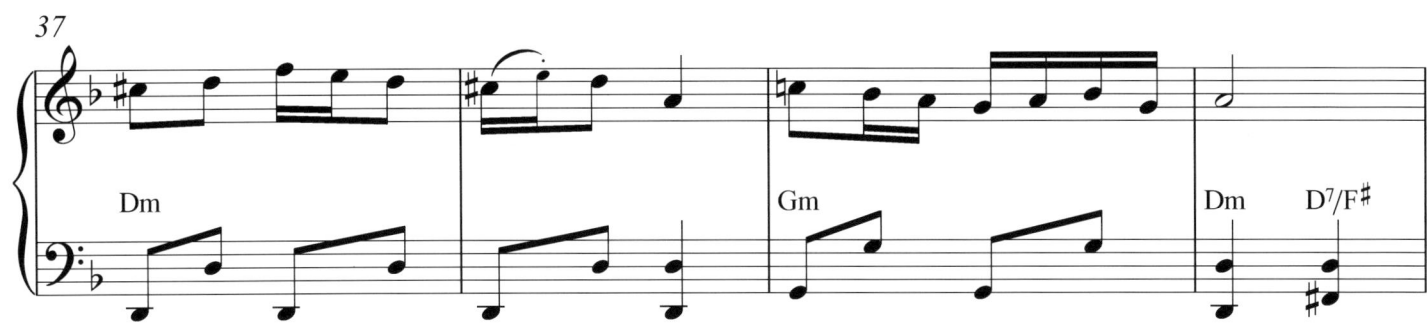

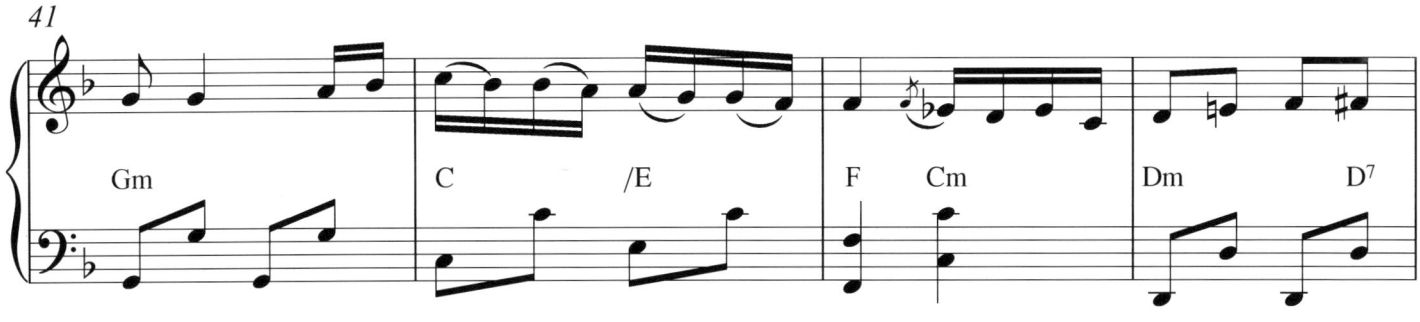

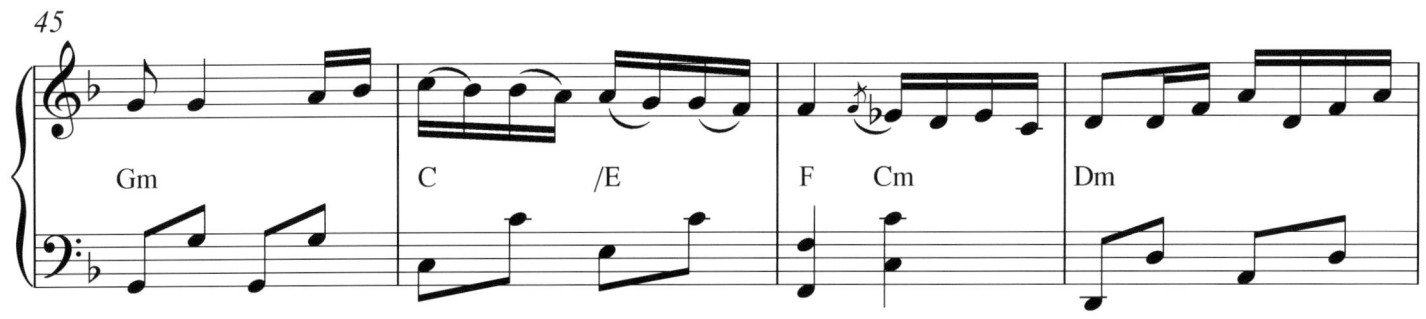

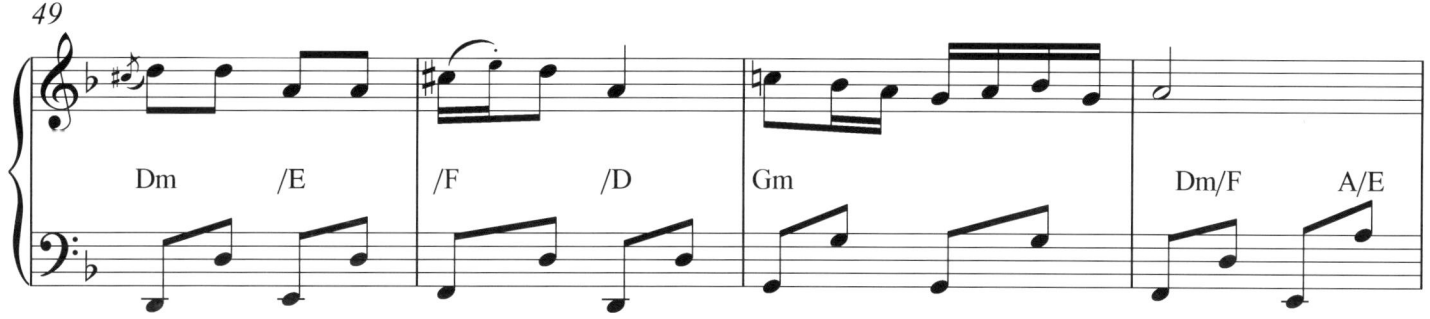

12

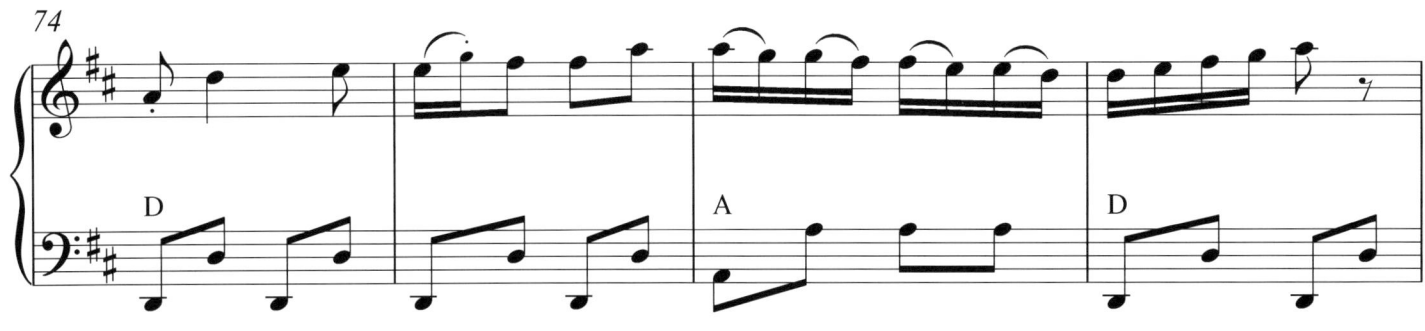

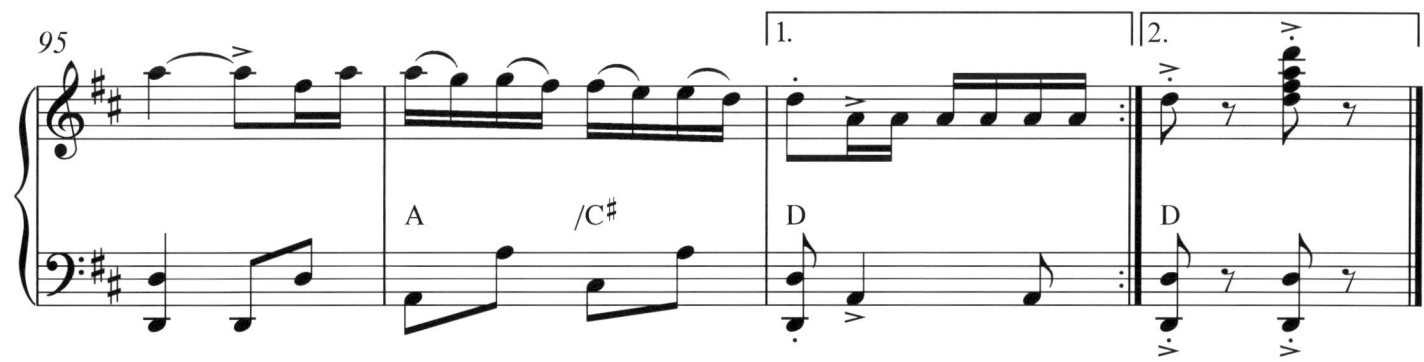

14

Dobridyen

Traditional
arr. Alan Bern

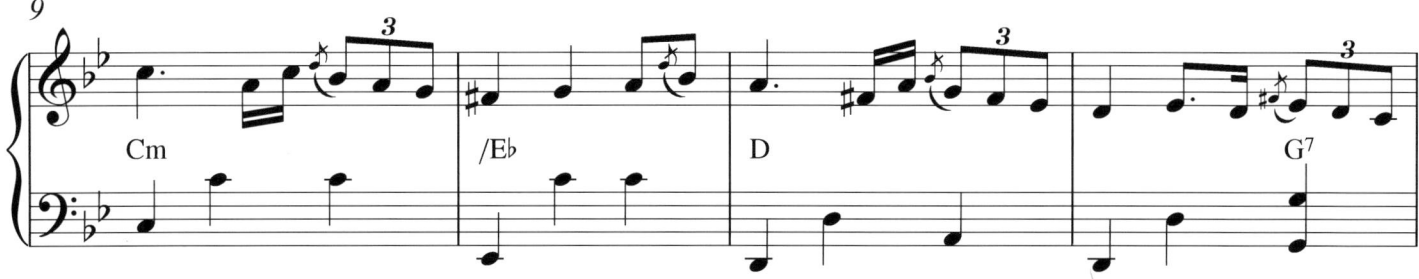

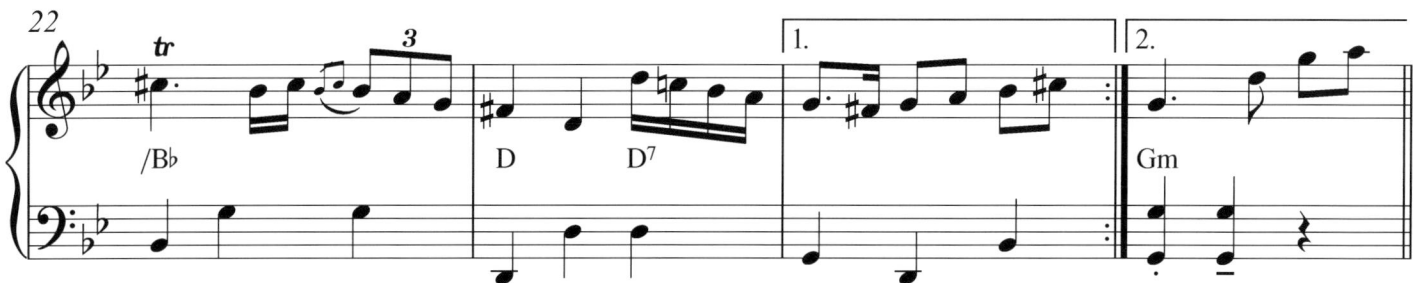

UE 36 122

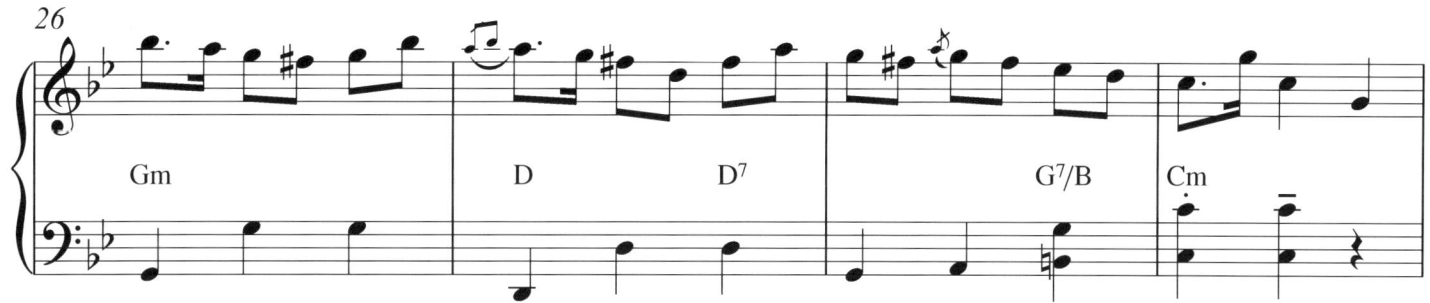

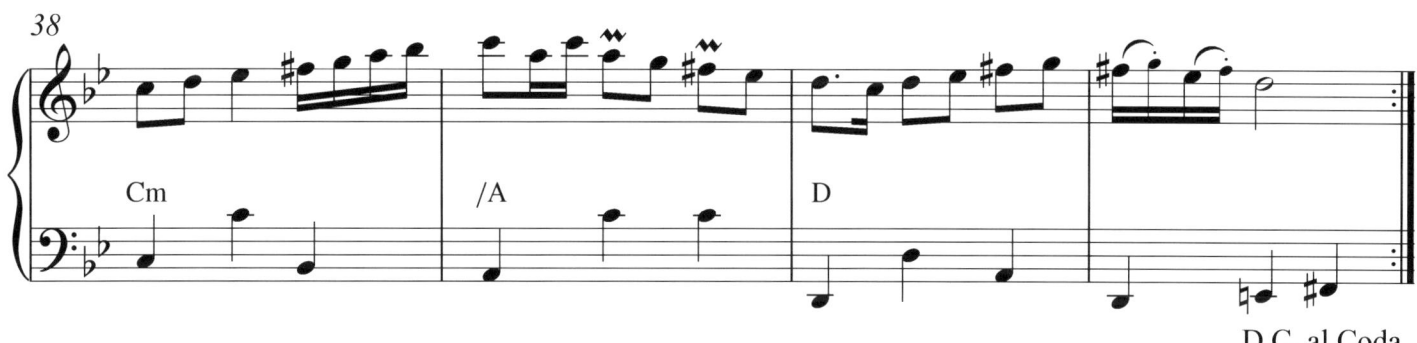

D.C. al Coda

Nakhes fun kinder

Traditional
arr. Alan Bern

Beachten Sie bitte, dass in diesem Stück d im Basssystem immer eine Bassnote ist und kein Akkord.
Note: In this piece, the D on the middle line of the bass staff is always a bass note, not a chord.
Note : dans cette pièce, le *ré* sur la ligne médiane de la portée de basse est toujours une note de basse, non un accord.

UE 36 122

Gas nign

Traditional
arr. Alan Bern

UE 36 122

Khupe tants

Traditional
arr. Alan Bern

UE 36 122

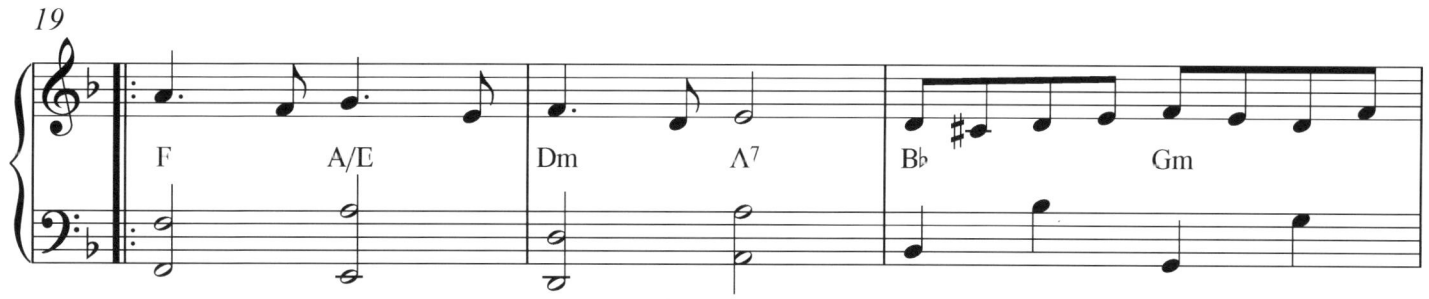

D.S. al Coda

Sha, sha di shviger kumt

Traditional
arr. Alan Bern

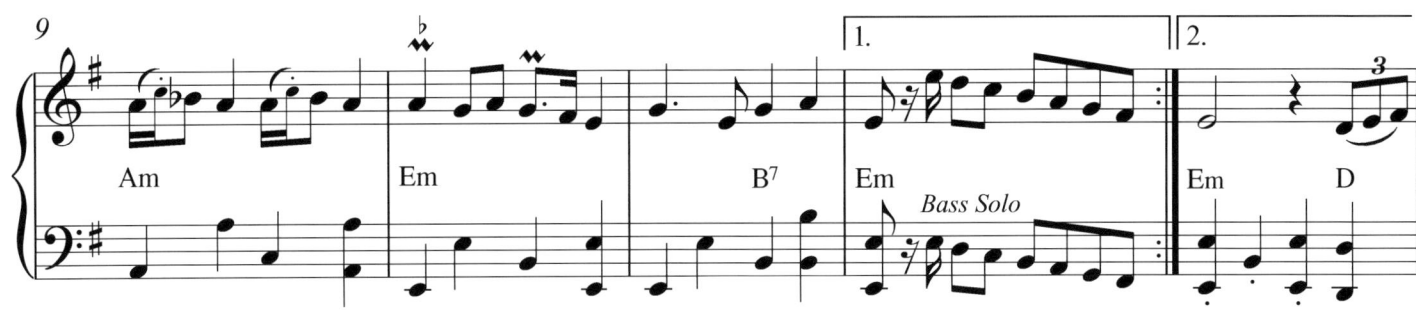

UE 36 122

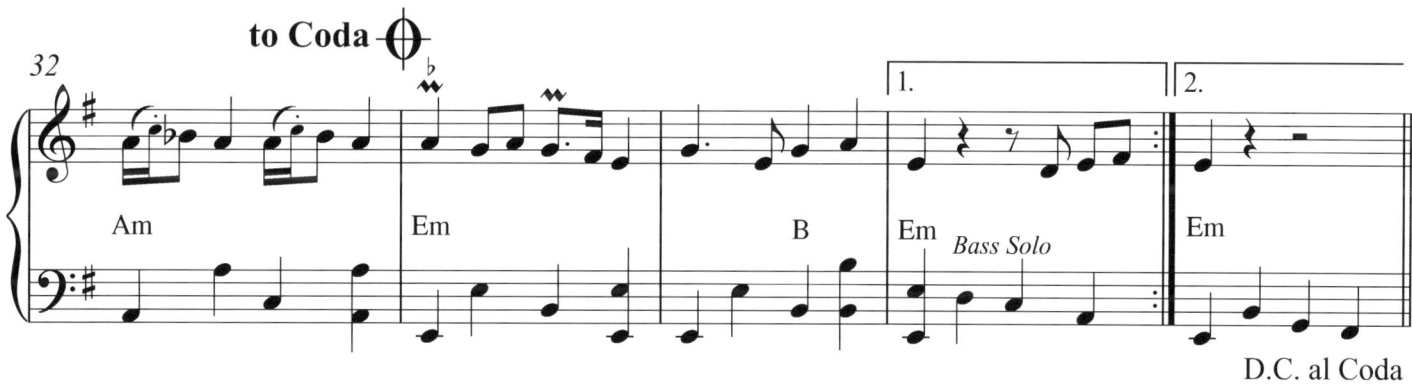

Dobranotsh

Traditional
arr. Alan Bern

UE 36 122

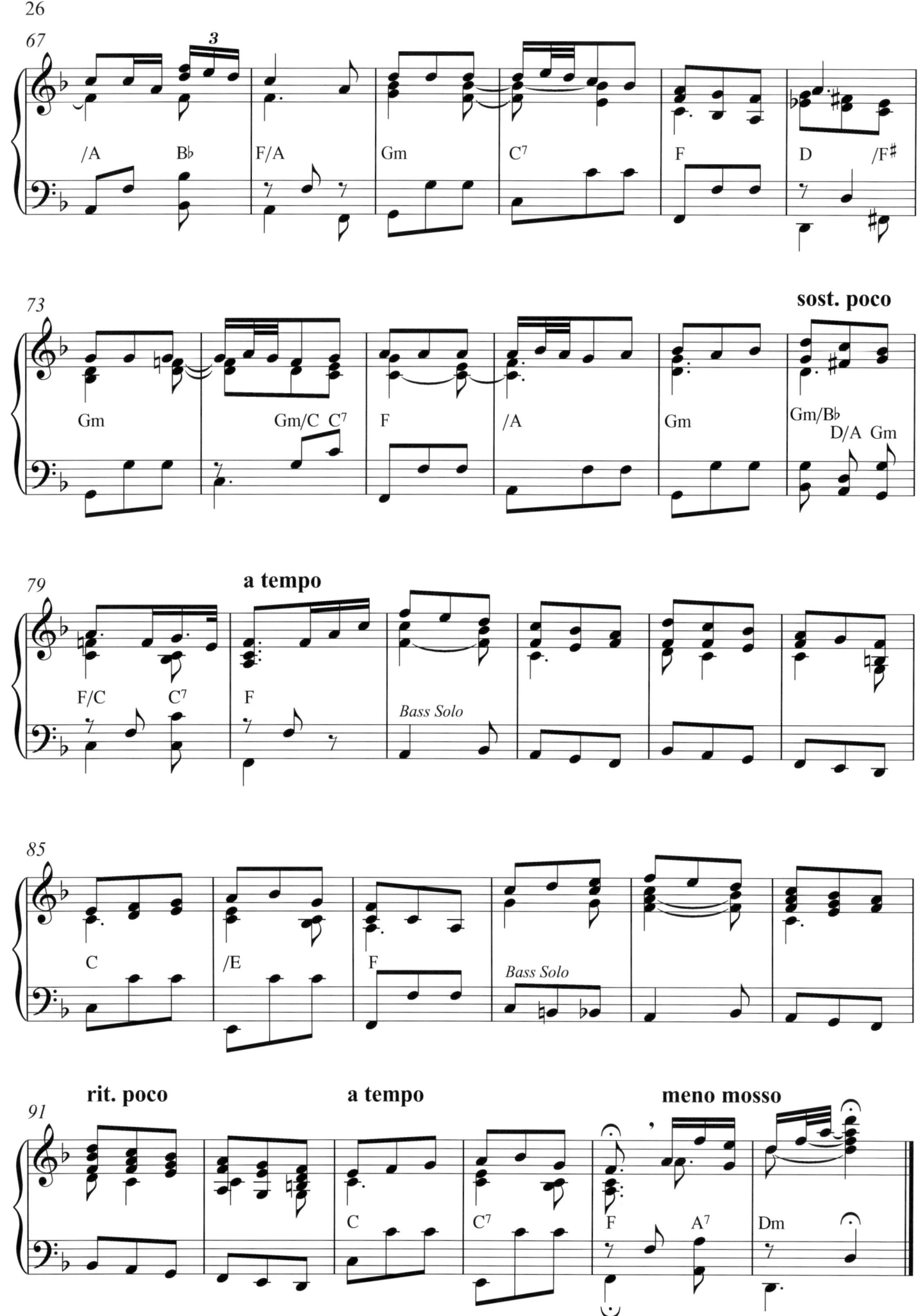

Bukusher Chusid

Traditional
arr. Alan Bern

UE 36 122

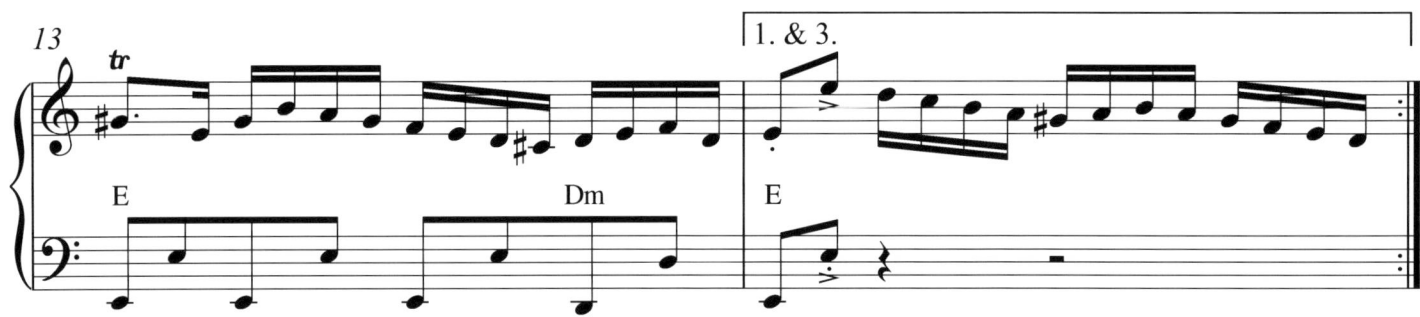

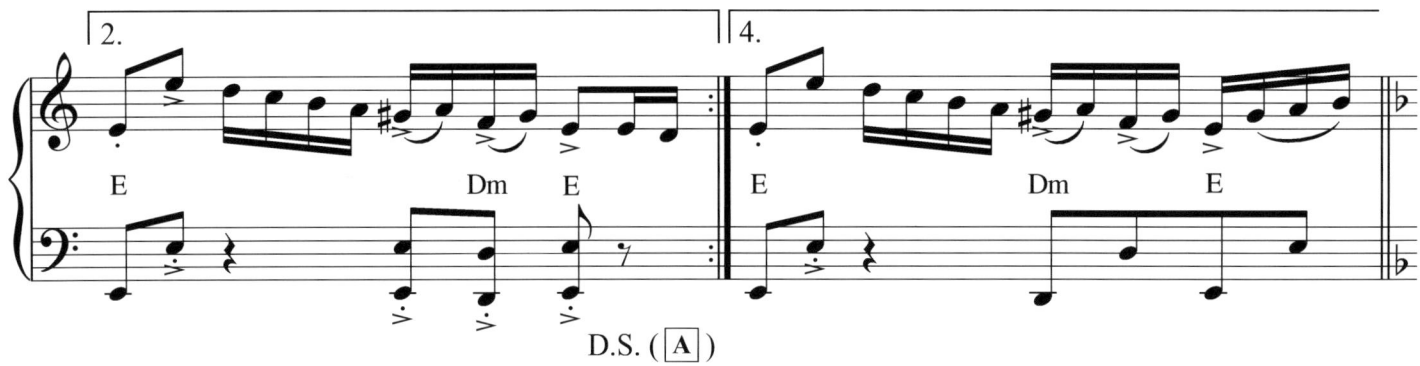

D.S. (A)

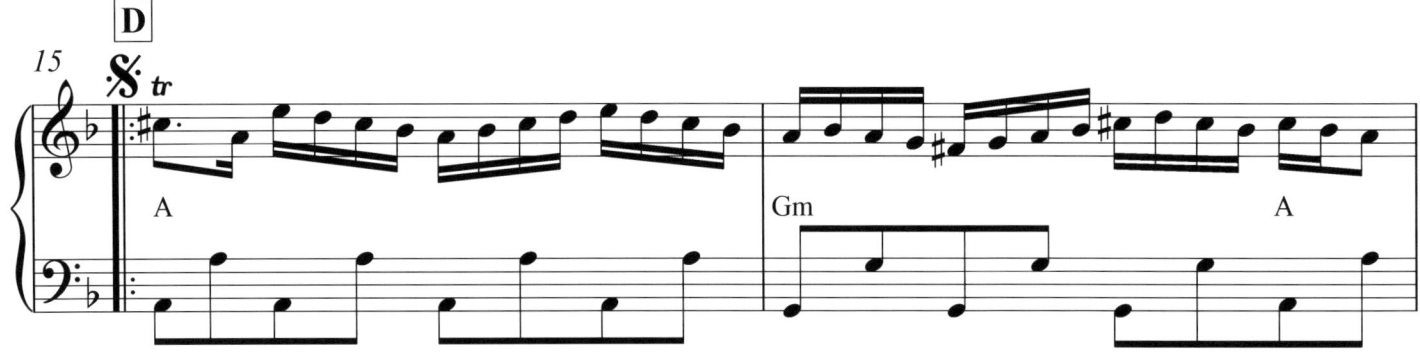

to Coda (on repeat)

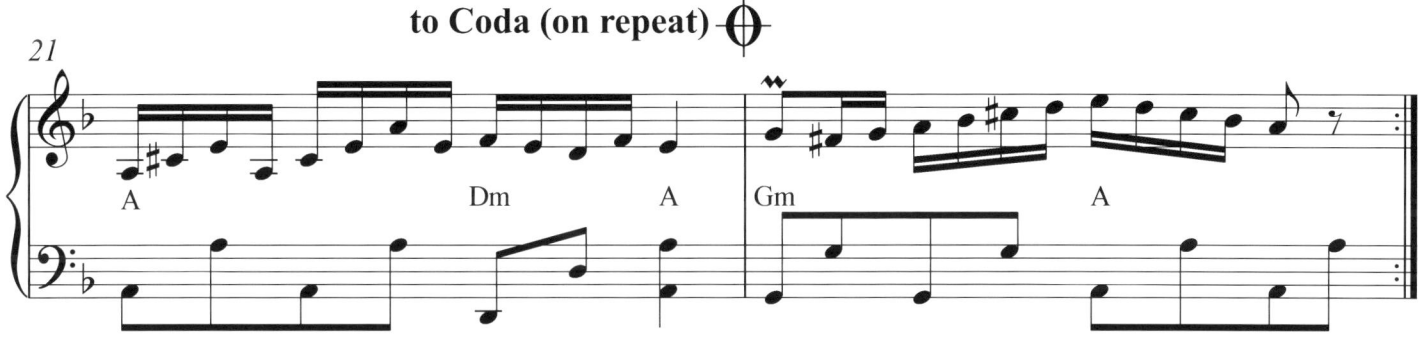

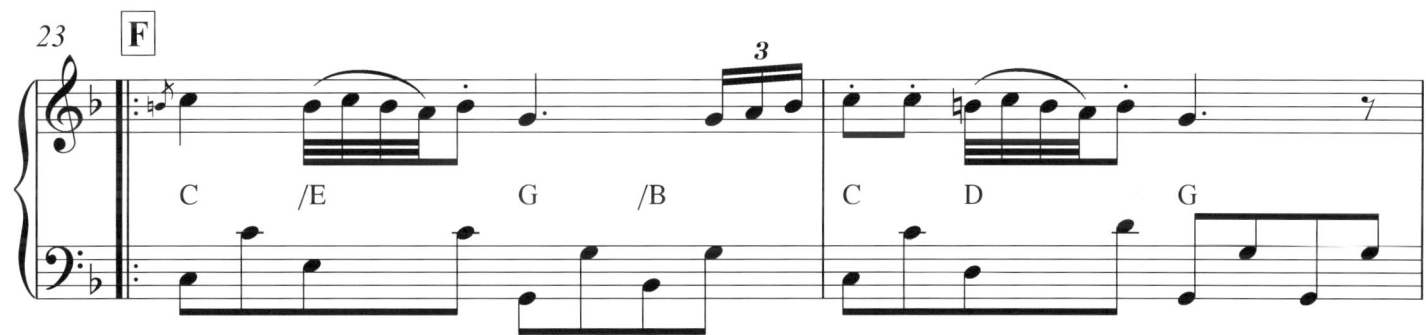

D.S. (D) al Coda

Coda

Terkishers

Traditional
arr. Alan Bern

UE 36 122

Odessa Bulgar

Traditional
arr. Alan Bern

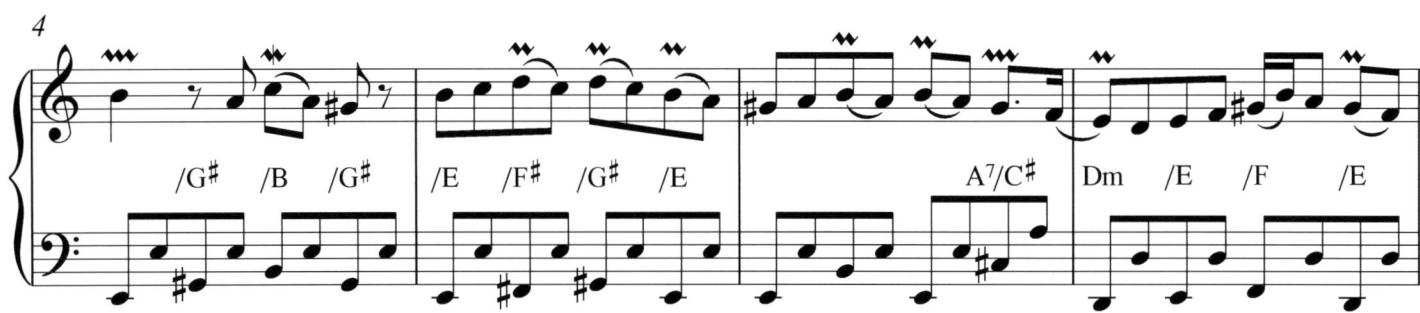

UE 36 122

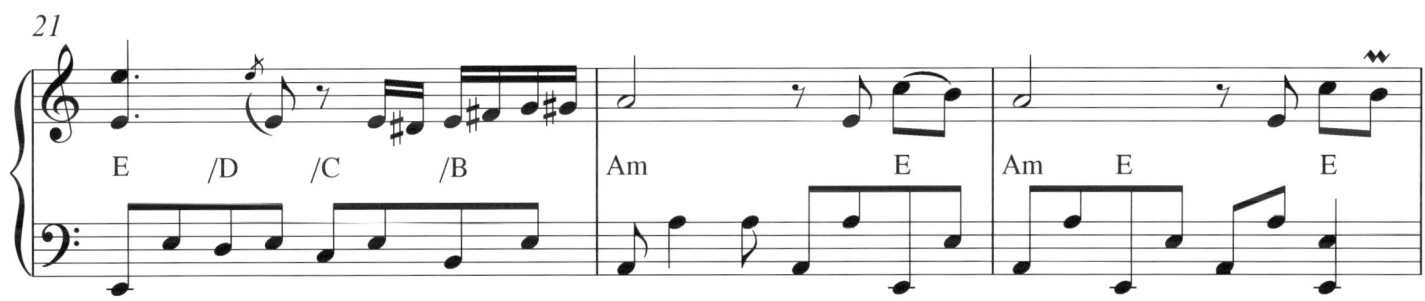

Koilen

Traditional

transcribed by Alan Bern

UE 36 122

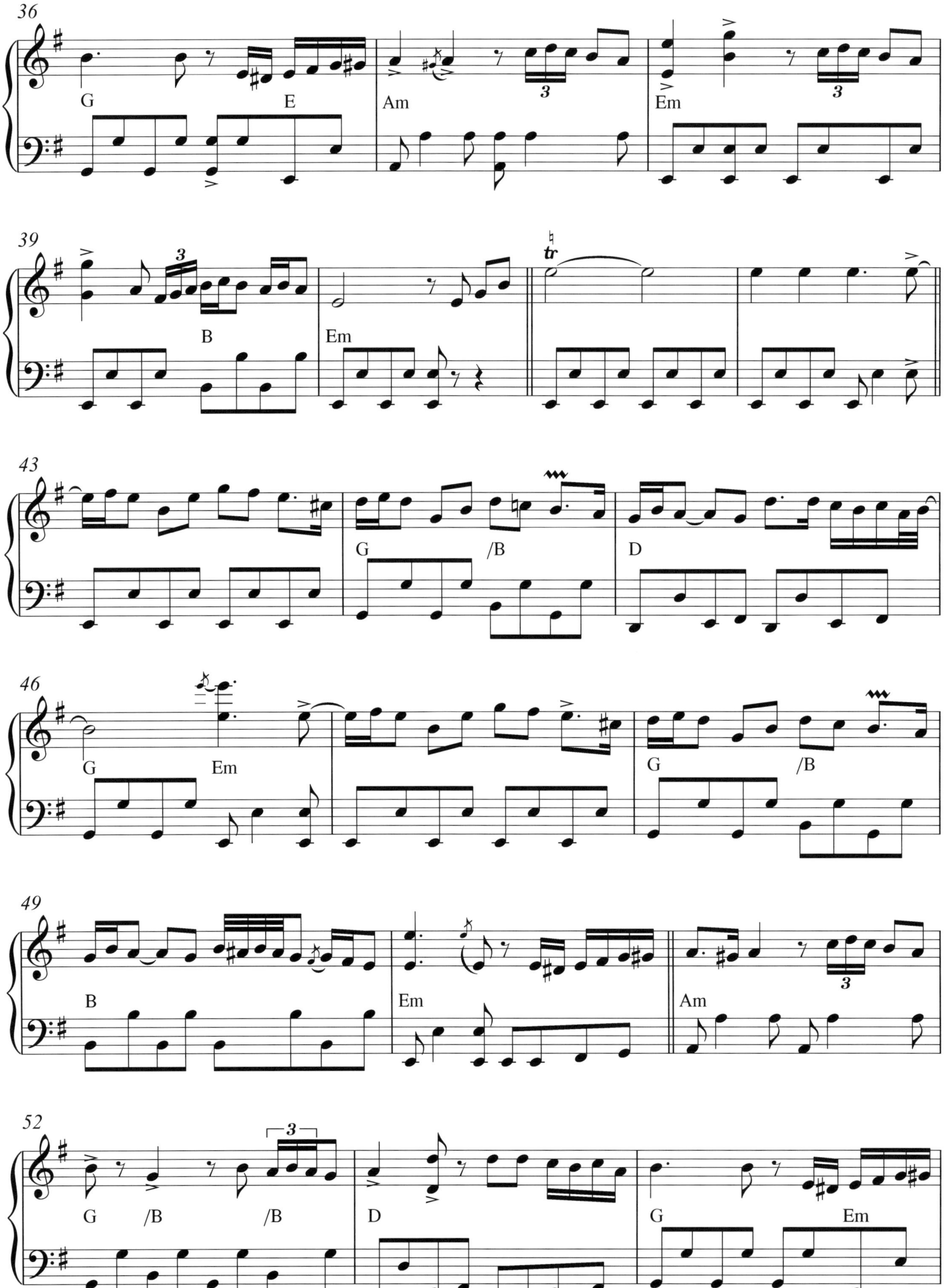
36
G E
Am
Em
39
B
Em
43
G /B
D
46
G Em
G /B
49
B
Em
Am
52
G /B /B
D
G Em

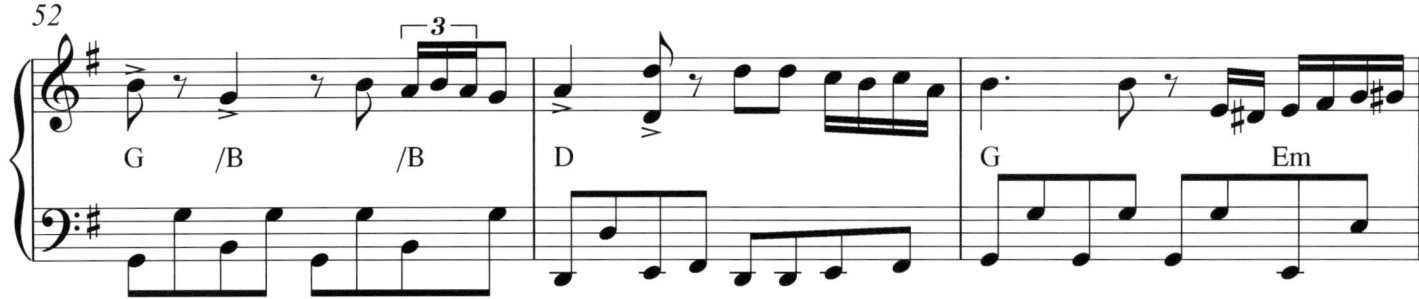

38

Anhang 1: Verzierung, Phrasierung und Bassnotation

Verzierung und Phrasierung

Unzählige Melodien des Klezmer-Repertoires finden sich in vielen weiteren Musiktraditionen, besonders in der griechischen, türkischen, rumänischen, ukrainischen und polnischen. Die Art und Weise, wie ein Klezmer-Musiker phrasiert und verziert, gibt den Melodien ihren klar abgrenzbaren jiddischen Charakter. Dieser stilistische Faktor ist aus der geschriebenen Musik nicht erkennbar. Eine Reihe ausgeschriebener Achtelnoten sagt wenig über deren rhythmische Empfindung und Phrasierung aus. Dies lässt sich in etwa mit ausnotierten Jazzmelodien vergleichen – *Swing* wird nicht notiert, und der Spieler muss diese Komponente bereits im Ohr haben. Die folgenden Beispiele befassen sich mit einigen generellen Phrasierungen und Verzierungensvarianten.

Generell sollten Noten ohne Bindebögen weder *legato* noch *staccato*, sondern abgesetzt gespielt werden. Paare gebundener Achtelnoten werden verdichtet und klingen fast wie Achteltriolen mit der Betonung auf der ersten und einer Pause auf der letzten Note. Dadurch wird der zu Grunde liegende Viertelnotenrhythmus deutlich.

Das gleiche Prinzip gilt auch für gebundene Sechzehntelpaare. Hier soll der zu Grunde liegende Achtelrhythmus hervortreten.

Gebundene Achteltriolen werden auch verdichtet und klingen fast wie drei gleiche Sechzehntel gefolgt von einer Sechzehntelpause. Dies hebt den zu Grunde liegenden Viertelnotenrhythmus hervor. Dasselbe gilt für gebundene Sechzehnteltriolen (nicht abgebildet), die wie drei Zweiunddreißigstel gefolgt von einer Zweiunddreißigstelpause klingen.

Das Prinzip des Verdichtens gilt sogar für gebundene Sechzehntel. Sie klingen etwa wie vier Noten einer Sechzehntelquintole gefolgt von einer Pause gleicher Länge. Dies hebt wiederum den zu Grunde liegenden Viertelrhythmus hervor.

Eine sehr charakteristische Klezmer-Verzierung ist der *krekhts*, den man hören muss, um ihn zu verstehen. Er klingt ein bisschen wie ein kleiner Schluckauf oder Seufzer. Für dieses Heft habe ich die untenstehende Notation eingeführt, um diese Verzierung erklären zu können. Sie zeigt zwei gebundene Sechzehntel. Die zweite davon hat einen kleineren Notenkopf und einen Staccatopunkt. Klanglich wird die erste Note akzentuiert und mit einem *legato* und *diminuendo* mit der zweiten Note verbunden, welche kaum zu hören ist. Dieser Absprung wird von einer kurzen Pause und danach einer sanften „Landung" auf der nächsten Note gefolgt. Typischerweise (aber nicht immer) liegt der *krekhts* einen Halbton unter der Landenote. Nach der zweiten Note muss vor der Landung auf der dritten Note eine Pause folgen! Fehlt diese, klingt das Resultat wie ein Doppelvorschlag und verliert den schluchzenden Effekt, der diese Verzierung so unverwechselbar macht.

Beim folgenden Beispiel handelt es sich auch um einen *krekhts*, diesmal ist jedoch die Ausgangsnote identisch mit der Zielnote. Diese Verzierung wird oft verwendet, um sich wiederholende Noten besonders expressiv und flehend klingen zu lassen.

Bassnotation

Es gibt viele verschiedene Möglichkeiten, die Noten für die linke Akkordeonseite zu notieren. Die nächsten Beispiele erläutern das in diesem Heft verwendete System.

Die Noten zwischen C und cis sind Bassnoten. Die Noten zwischen e und dis' repräsentieren Akkorde. Die Noten d und dis können je nach musikalischem Kontext entweder Bass- oder Akkordnoten sein.

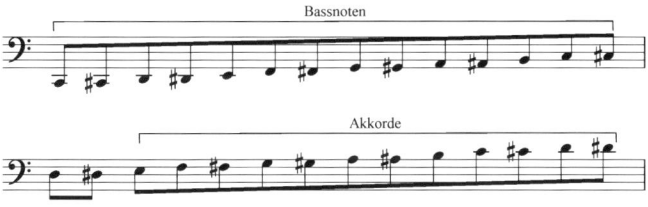

Dies ist ein Beispiel für das oben erklärte Prinzip. Anstatt alle Stimmen zu notieren, werden die Akkorde durch ihre Grundtöne dargestellt (A ist beispielsweise der Grundton von A-Dur oder a-Moll). Diese Schreibweise hat zwei Vorteile: Sie ist einfach zu lesen und funktioniert für alle Standardbassakkordeons unabhängig von instrumentenbedingten Differenzen in Stimmführung und Register.

Wenn eine Bassnote und ein Akkord gleichzeitig statt abwechselnd erklingen, werden sie wie die Offbeat-Noten in diesem Beispiel notiert.

Bei der Notation mehrerer einzelner Bassnoten nacheinander erscheint es manchmal aus visueller Sicht sinnvoll, die obere Hälfte des Notensystems zu verwenden, obwohl dieser Teil normalerweise Akkorden und nicht Bassnoten vorbehalten ist. In diesen Fällen sind die entsprechenden Passagen mit der Bezeichnung *Bass Solo* gekennzeichnet.

Wenn im Bass eines Akkords nicht der Grundton steht, folgt in der Akkordbezeichnung auf den Akkordnamen ein Schrägstrich und die entsprechende Bassnote. Hier finden Sie vier Beispiele dafür. Sie sehen, dass der D-Dur Akkord im dritten Beispiel über dem System notiert ist, während im vierten Beispiel derselbe Akkord auf der Mittellinie des Systems wiederkehrt. Dies verhindert, dass Akkorde und Bassnoten zu eng aneinander oder mit zu großem Abstand notiert werden.

Wenn die Bassnote wechselt, während der Akkord wiederholt wird, so wird der Akkord nicht jedes Mal neu notiert. Stattdessen zeigt ein Schrägstrich gefolgt vom entsprechenden Bassnotennamen die wechselnde Bassnote unter einem sich wiederholenden Akkord.

Alle Bassnoten und Akkorde wurden nach internationalem Standard bezeichnet: B = H, F♯ = Fis, E♭ = Es.

Anhang 2: Zu den Stücken

Dieses Stück im *freygish*-Stil ist ein perfekt konzipiertes Beispiel des jiddischen *hora*-Genre im Dreiertakt, welches sich durch eine subtile Balance zwischen Gesanglichkeit und Rhythmik auszeichnet. Es steht am Anfang dieser Sammlung, denn es ist technisch leicht zu meistern und zeigt, dass emotionale Tiefe keiner komplexen Harmonik bedarf. Da es sich bei der *hora* um Tanzmusik handelt, sollte die Begleitung gleichmäßig aber nicht starr sein.

Diese schöne Melodie ist ein weiteres Beispiel einer *hora* im Dreiertakt. Sie wurde unter anderem vom Violinisten Max Leibowitz als *Yiddish tants* aufgenommen. Unter Klezmer-Musikern ist das Stück heute als *Kandel's hora* bekannt. Wie auch die *D-freygish hora* verwendet diese Bearbeitung nur drei Akkorde, um nicht von der Expressivität der Melodie abzulenken.

Diese Melodie wurde ursprünglich als *hora #159*, in Petru Stoianovs großartiger Sammlung *500 melodii de jocuri din Moldova* (500 Melodien aus Moldawien), Chisinau: Cartea Moldoveneasca, 1972 veröffentlicht. Das Stück repräsentiert nur einen von verschiedenen Typen der moldawischen *hora*. Es ist technisch nicht sehr schwer, aber emotional nuanciert.

Diese Suite kombiniert drei fröhliche Tanzmelodien. Die erste ist *#182, zhok*, aus Stoianovs Sammlung von 1972 (siehe auch *Moldavian Yiddish Hora*), die zweite (ab Buchstabe B) ist eine traditionelle Melodie, bekannt als *Jokul lui Tudoska* (*Tudoskas zhok*) und die dritte (ab Buchstabe C) ein traditionelles moldawisches *sher*. Das Tempo kann zu Beginn jedes neuen Stückes leicht gesteigert werden, sollte aber bis zum Ende beschwingt bleiben.

Ein *dobridyen* (Guten Morgen) ist ein Musikstück, das Gäste auf Hochzeiten oder anderen Festlichkeiten begrüßt. Die Melodie ist sehr gefühlvoll. Das Tempo sollte flexibel bleiben und dem Atemrhythmus der melodischen Phrasierung folgen.

Diese Bearbeitung basiert auf einer Aufnahme, die im frühen 20. Jahrhundert in Polen mit dem unverwechselbaren *Belfs Romanian Orchestra* entstand. Der Titel bedeutet soviel wie „stolz auf die Kinder sein". Die Melodie dieser Bearbeitung ist technisch nicht sehr anspruchsvoll; jedoch ist es eine Herausforderung, Bass und Akkorde mit Gefühl und wie im Zwiegespräch mit der Mclodie zu spielen. Das Tempo sollte gleichmäßig, aber nicht starr sein.

Ein *gas nign* wurde von *klezmorim* gespielt, um Menschen von einem Ort zum anderen mit Musik zu begleiten. Das Stück ist in Ausdruck und Tempo moderat und feierlich. Trotzdem wird dieses Stück wohl überraschen, denn es scheint eine Kreuzung aus Barockelementen und jiddischer Musik zu sein, die manchmal mit jeder Phrase wechseln. Diese Bearbeitung betont besonders die in der Melodie implizierte Harmonik, obwohl es sehr unwahrscheinlich ist, dass das Stück in der Vergangenheit auf diese Weise gespielt wurde. Die Bass- und Akkordstimmen sollten weich fließen und die expressive Freiheit der Melodie nicht behindern.

Der *Khupe tants* (Baldachin-Tanz) aus einer Aufnahme aus dem frühen 20. Jahrhundert von Abe Schwartz hat ein besonderes jiddisches Flair und unterscheidet sich somit deutlich von der Musik anderer osteuropäischer Länder sowie der des Balkans. Die gebundenen Achtelnoten sollten verdichtet werden (siehe *Anhang 1: Verzierung, Phrasierung und Bassnotation*), und das Stück ein bisschen, aber nicht übertrieben schwerfällig gespielt werden.

Diese Melodie wurde erstmals 1912 vom *Belfs Rumänisches Orchester* als *Dem Rebns Gavdule* (Die Havdole des Rabbiners) aufgenommen. Die bekanntere Einspielung ist jedoch *Sha, sha di shviger kumt* (Still, still, die Schwiegermutter kommt) des Klarinettisten Dave Tarras (1897–1989). Tarras, dessen lange Karriere fast das ganze 20. Jahrhundert andauerte, nahm das Stück im frühen 20. Jahrhundert auf, noch bevor die schnellen *bulgars* in Amerika so beliebt wurden, die das ältere Repertoire praktisch verdrängten. In den letzten 20 Jahren wurde Dave Tarras Aufnahme mehrmals wiederveröffentlicht.

Dobranotsh

Ein *dobranotsh* (Gute Nacht) ist ein Abschlussstück, das für Gäste gespielt wird, die nach einer Hochzeit oder einem anderen großen Fest nach Hause aufbrechen. Es ist das siebente Stück in Moshe Beregovskis Monumentalwerk *Jewish Instrumental Folk Music*, 1937, das 2001 von *Syracuse University Press* neu aufgelegt wurde. Beregovski komponierte das Stück im 3/4-Takt im Tempo ♩ = 132. Mir gefällt ein etwas langsameres Tempo im 3/8-Takt. Das Stück sollte sehr singend gespielt werden – Melodie und Harmonik geben dabei den Fluss der Musik und den Atemrhythmus vor. Bis Takt 48 sind Harmonik und Begleitung eher schlicht gehalten. Der Spieler kann das Stück vom Anfang wiederholen und mit Takt 48 schließen, oder dem Verlauf des Stückes bis zum Ende folgen, wo die harmonische Begleitung deutlich komplexer und moderner wird.

Bukusher Chusid

Der in Rumänien geborene Zymbalvirtuose Joseph Moskowitz (1879–1954) ließ sich später in New York nieder. Seine wunderbaren Einspielungen sind Bestandteil vieler neuaufgelegter Klezmer-Compilations, und seine Stücke werden auch heute noch von Klezmer-Musikern gerne gespielt. Diese Bearbeitung für Akkordeon ist technisch anspruchsvoll und verlangt eine leichte Spieltechnik in der rechten Hand.

Terkishers

Der *terkisher* zeichnet sich durch akzentuierte rhythmische Muster aus, die für die darüber liegende Melodie ein solides Gerüst bilden sollten. Diese Suite kombiniert zwei Stücke, die vom berühmten Klezmer-Klarinettisten Naftule Brandwein (1884–1963) unter den Namen *Ziser Bulgar* (Süßer Bulgar) und *Fufzehn yahr fon der heim awek* (Fünfzehn Jahre weg von zu Hause) aufgenommen wurden. Die Herausforderung für den Akkordeonisten ist dabei, die freie Phrasierung und Rhythmik in der Melodie beizubehalten, ohne die Begleitung durcheinanderzubringen.

Odessa Bulgar

Dieses Stück aus Mishka Ziganoffs Repertoire (siehe auch *Koilen*) ist vielmehr eine Bearbeitung als eine Transkription einer Aufnahme. Es lebt vom Zusammenspiel der Akzente zwischen Melodie und Begleitung. Die Akzente sollten jedoch nicht

allzu schwer sein, damit der Gesamtausdruck beschwingt bleibt. Ziganoffs eigene Aufnahme ist auf YouTube zu finden.

Koilen

Der berühmte Klezmer-Akkordeonist Mishka Ziganoff (1889–1967) hat viele Aufnahmen eingespielt und sein schwebender, rhythmischer Stil ist das häufigste Vorbild für die meisten Klezmer-Akkordeonisten heute. Das Stück ist eine relativ getreue Transkription seiner Aufnahme des jiddischen Volksliedes *Koilen* und ein ausgezeichnetes Beispiel für Ziganoffs Stil: Melodie und Begleitung werden minimal aber effektiv variiert, so dass jede Wiederholung des Themas spannend bleibt. Dieses Stück ist für diejenigen beigefügt, die sich intensiver mit Ziganoffs einzigartigem Stil befassen möchten. Die Einspielung kann auch auf YouTube gefunden werden.

Anmerkung: Mehrere Stücke der Sammlung (*Moldavian Yiddish Hora*, *Moldavian Yiddish Suite*, *Sha, sha di shviger kumt* und *Terkishers*) sind auch auf der CD *Splendor* der Gruppe *The Other Europeans* zu hören.

Appendix 1: Ornamentation, Phrasing and Bass Staff Notation

Ornamentation and Phrasing

Many melodies in the klezmer repertoire also exist in Greek, Turkish, Romanian, Ukrainian, Polish and other musical traditions. The way a klezmer musician phrases and ornaments goes a long way to giving a melody its distinctive Yiddish flavor. This stylistic level is not at all obvious from the written music. A string of written eighth-notes doesn't tell us much about their rhythmic feel and phrasing. You can compare this with notated jazz melodies - the *swing* isn't written out, it's something you have to already have in your ear. The following examples briefly discuss some basic, characteristic phrasing and ornamentation.

In general, notes without slurs should be played neither *legato* nor *staccato* – but detached. Pairs of slurred eighth-notes are 'squeezed together' a bit and sound closer to eighth-note triplets with an accent on the first note and a rest on the third. The effect is to bring out the underlying quarter-note rhythm.

The same principle holds for pairs of slurred sixteenth-notes, which brings out the underlying eighth-note rhythm.

Slurred eighth-note triplets are also 'squeezed' to sound more like three even sixteenth-notes followed by a sixteenth-note rest. This also brings out the underlying quarter-note rhythmic level. The same principle applies to slurred sixteenth-note triplets (not shown here), which sound like three thirty-second-notes followed by a thirty-second-note rest.

The 'squeezing' principle even applies to four slurred sixteenth-notes! They sound something like four notes in a sixteenth-note quintuplet followed by a rest of the same length. Again, this brings out the underlying quarter-note rhythm.

Very likely the most characteristic klezmer ornament is the *krekhts*, which must be heard to be understood. It's a little like a hiccup or a sob. For this book, I've invented the notation below to show this ornament. It shows two slurred sixteenths, the second of which has a smaller notehead and a *staccato*. In sound, the first note is accented, connected by *legato* and *diminuendo* to the second note, which is barely heard. This 'take-off' is followed by a brief rest and then a soft 'landing' on the next note. In the classic situation, the *krekhts* is played on a note one-half step below the 'landing' tone. There must be a rest following the second note before landing on the third note! If not, then the result sounds like a double grace note and loses the quality of sobbing that makes this ornament so distinctive.

This is also a *krekhts*, but on a repeated note, instead of below the 'goal' note. It is very common as a way of making repeated notes sound expressive and pleading.

Bass Staff Notation

There are many different approaches to notation for the left side of the accordion. The next examples explain the system used in this book.

The notes written from C below the staff to C♯ on the staff represent bass notes. The notes written from E on the staff to D♯ above the staff represent chords. The notes D and D♯ on the middle line of the staff can represent either bass notes or chords, depending on the context:

Here is an example of the principles explained above. Instead of writing out all of its voices, a chord is represented by its root note (for example, A is the root of A major or minor). This system has two advantages: it is easier to read, and it works for all standard bass accordions, regardless of differences in chord voicing and registration from one instrument to the next.

When a bass note and a chord are played simultaneously instead of alternating, they are notated like the off-beats in this example.

When notating a run of individual bass notes, sometimes it is visually intuitive to use the upper half of the staff, even though it's usually reserved for chords instead of individual bass notes. In such cases, the words *Bass Solo* appear above or below the passage.

If a chord has a bass note other than its own root, the chord name is followed by a slash followed by the bass note. Here are four cases. Notice that in the third case, the D chord is notated above the staff, and in the fourth case the same chord is notated on the middle line of the staff. This avoids the chords and bass notes being written either too close together or too far apart on the staff.

If the bass note changes but the chord is repeated, rather than notating the chord each time, a slash followed by a bass note name shows the changing bass note under an unchanging chord.

Appendix 2: Notes on the pieces

This piece in the *freygish* mode is a perfectly constructed example of the Yiddish, triple-meter *hora* genre, beautifully balanced between lyricism and rhythm. It has an early place in this collection because it is not technically difficult and it shows that a melody doesn't have to have complex harmony to be deeply touching. Because a *hora* is dance music, the accompaniment should be steady but not rigid.

Another example of a Yiddish, triple-meter *hora*, this beautiful melody was also recorded by violinist Max Leibowitz as *Yiddish tants* and many others. It is popularly known among klezmer musicians today as *Kandel's Hora*. Like the *D-freygish Hora*, this setting uses only three chords so as not to distract from the expressiveness of the melody.

This melody was published as *hora #159*, in Petru Stoianov's great collection *500 melodii de jocuri din Moldova* (500 Joc melodies from Moldova), Chisinau: Cartea Moldoveneasca, 1972. It represents one of several different kinds of Moldavian *horas*. It is technically not difficult, but emotionally subtle.

This suite puts together three joyous dance tunes. The first is *#182, zhok*, from Stoianov's 1972 collection (see also *Moldavian Yiddish Hora*), the second (at rehearsal mark B) is a traditional tune known as *Jokul lui Tudoska* (Tudoska's zhok), and the third (at rehearsal mark C) a traditional Moldavian *sher*. The tempo can get slightly faster at the beginning of each new piece, but it should stay bouncy to the end.

A *dobridyen* (meaning 'good morning') is music played to greet guests at weddings or other festive events. The melody is very lyrical and the tempo should be flexible and 'breathing', following the melodic phrasing.

This arrangement is based on a recording made in early 20th century Poland by the idiosyncratic *Belf's Romanian Orchestra*. The title means a 'feeling of pride in one's children'. The melody in this arrangement is not technically difficult, but playing the

bass and chords with feeling and in dialogue with the melody is a challenge. The tempo should be steady but not rigid.

A *gas nign* was played by *klezmorim* to accompany people walking from one place to another and it has a stately, moderate tempo and character. Nevertheless, this piece may surprise the player as a hybrid that seems to combine baroque and Yiddish music, sometimes changing phrase-by-phrase. The arrangement here fully exploits the implied harmonies of the melody, although it is very unlikely that it was ever played this way in the past. The bass and chord voices should flow smoothly and not hold back the expressive freedom of the melody.

From an early 20th century recording by Abe Schwartz, *Khupe tants* (Wedding Canopy Dance), this has a very special Yiddish flavor that sets it far apart from other Eastern European or Balkan music. The slurred eighth-notes should be squeezed together (see *Appendix 1: Ornamentation and Phrasing*) and the rhythmic feeling should be slightly lumbering but not too heavy.

This melody was first recorded by *Belf's Romanian Orchestra* in 1912 as *Dem Rebns Gavdule* (The rabbi's havdole) but the more well-known recording by clarinetist Dave Tarras (1897–1989) was called *Sha, sha di shviger kumt* (Quiet, quiet, the mother-in-law is coming). Tarras, whose career spanned almost the entire 20th century, recorded this piece in the early 20th century before the fast-tempo *bulgars* became so popular in America to the virtual exclusion of older repertoires. In the last 20 years, Tarras' recording has been re-issued many times.

A *dobranotsh* (meaning 'good night') is music played for guests departing after a wedding or other festive event. It is the seventh tune in Moshe Beregovski's monumental *Jewish Instrumental Folk Music*, 1937, reprinted in 2001 by *Syracuse University Press*. Beregovski notates the piece in 3/4 with ♩ = 132. I prefer a slightly slower tempo notated in 3/8. This piece should be played very smoothly with all of the breath and lilt implied by the melody and harmony. Through bar 48, the harmony and accompaniment is kept rather simple. The player can repeat from the beginning and end at bar 48, or continue through the more complex and modern harmonic accompaniment, as written, to the end of the piece.

Bukusher Chusid **27**
Joseph Moskowitz (1879–1954) was a Romanian-born cymbalom virtuoso who eventually settled in New York. His many wonderful recordings are favorite tracks on many klezmer music re-issues and his tunes remain beloved among today's klezmer musicians. This arrangement for accordion is technically challenging and requires a light touch.

Terkishers **30**
The *terkisher* is distinguished by its strong rhythmic pattern, which should remain a steady base for the melody on top of it. This suite combines two tunes recorded by the great klezmer clarinetist, Naftule Brandwein (1884–1963), which he called *Ziser Bulgar* (Sweet bulgar) and *Fufzehn yahr fon der heim awek* (Fifteen years away from home). The challenge for an accordionist is to have great rhythmic and lyrical freedom in the melody without shaking up the accompaniment.

Odessa Bulgar **32**
From the repertoire of Mishka Ziganoff (see also *Koilen*), this piece is an arrangement rather than a transcription of a recording. It lives from the interplay of accents between the melody and accompaniment, and the basic sound must be light so that the accents don't become too heavy. Ziganoff's own recording can be heard on YouTube.

Koilen **34**
The great klezmer accordionist Mishka Ziganoff (1889–1967) made many recordings and his light, rhythmic style remains the dominant model for most klezmer accordionists today. This piece is a close transcription of his 1919 recording of the Yiddish folk song *Koilen*. It's an excellent example of how he plays small but meaningful variations in the melody and accompaniment so that each repetition of the tune remains fascinating. It's included here for those who would like to dig deeper into Ziganoff's unique style and it can be heard on YouTube.

Note – several pieces in this collection (*Moldavian Yiddish Hora, Moldavian Yiddish Suite, Sha, sha di shviger kumt* and *Terkishers*) can be heard on *The Other Europeans' Splendor* CD.

Annexe 1: Ornementation, Phrasé et Notation de la basse

Ornementation et Phrasé

Beaucoup de mélodies du répertoire klezmer existent aussi dans la musique populaire grecque, turque, roumaine, ukrainienne, polonaise etc. Le phrasé et les ornements contribuent énormément à rendre une mélodie typiquement yiddish. Or, ce niveau stylistique est très peu rendu par la partition. Une série de croches ne nous en dit pas beaucoup sur le phrasé ou sur le balancement rythmique. C'est un peu comme pour les mélodies de jazz : le « swing » n'est pas noté, il faut l'avoir dans l'oreille. Les exemples qui suivent reviennent brièvement sur quelques phrasés et ornements de base.

En général, les notes non liées ne devraient être jouées ni *legato* ni *staccato*, mais détachées. Les croches liées par deux sont légèrement « resserrées » et sonnent un peu comme des triolets de croches avec un accent sur la première note et un silence sur la troisième. Cela fait ressortir le rythme en noires sous-jacent.

Le même principe s'applique aux doubles croches liées par deux, ce qui fait ressortir le rythme en croches sous-jacent.

Les triolets de croches liées sont aussi « resserrés », pour sonner davantage comme trois doubles égales suivies d'un quart de soupir. Là encore, cela a pour effet de mettre en valeur le niveau rythmique sous-jacent, à la noire. Il en va de même pour les triolets de doubles croches liées (non montrés ici), qui sonnent davantage comme trois triples croches suivies d'un huitième de soupir.

Le principe du « resserrement » s'applique même aux quatre doubles liées ! Elles évoquent plutôt les quatre premières notes d'un quintuplet de doubles suivies d'un silence de même durée. Le but est toujours de faire ressortir le rythme en noires sous-jacent.

Le *krekhts* est certainement l'ornement le plus typique du klezmer. Il faut l'entendre pour le comprendre : il ressemble un peu à un hoquet ou à un sanglot. Pour lui, j'ai inventé pour ce recueil la notation ci-dessous. Il s'agit de deux doubles liées dont la seconde est plus petite et notée *staccato*. La première note est accentuée et liée par un *legato* et un *diminuendo* à la seconde note, à peine audible. Ce « décollage » est suivi d'un bref silence et d'un subtil « atterrissage » sur la note suivante. Classiquement, les *krekhts* sont joués sur une note un-demi ton en dessous de la note « d'atterrissage ». Il doit y avoir un silence entre la deuxième note et la troisième ! Sinon, on aura une sorte de double appoggiature et on perdra l'effet de sanglot qui donne tout son caractère à cet ornement.

Il s'agit également d'un *krekhts*, mais sur une note répétée et non inférieure à la note « cible ». Il est très fréquent pour donner un ton insistant et expressif à des notes répétées.

Notation de la basse

La notation de la main gauche de l'accordéon fait l'objet de nombreuses approches différentes. Les six exemples qui suivent expliquent le système adopté dans ce recueil.

Les notes allant du *do* sous la portée au *do* dièse sur la portée représentent la basse. Du *mi* sur la portée au *ré* dièse au-dessus de la portée, ce sont les accords. Les notes *ré* et *ré* dièse au milieu de la portée peuvent appartenir à la basse ou aux accords, en fonction du contexte.

Voici un exemple des principes exposés ci-dessus. Au lieu d'écrire toutes les voix, je représente les accords par leur fondamentale (par exemple, *la* pour l'accord de *la* majeur ou mineur). Ce système a deux avantages : il est plus facile à lire et il fonctionne pour tous les accordéons chromatiques standard, indépendamment des différences de registres et de disposition des accords d'un instrument à l'autre.

Lorsqu'une note de basse et un accord sont joués simultanément et non l'un après l'autre, ils sont notés comme les contre-temps sur cet exemple.

Lorsqu'on représente une suite de notes de basse, il est parfois plus intuitif d'utiliser la partie supérieure de la portée, même si elle est habituellement réservée aux accords. Dans ce cas, les mots *Bass Solo* sont écrits au-dessus ou en dessous du passage.

Si un accord a une note de basse autre que sa fondamentale, le nom de l'accord est suivi d'une barre oblique, puis de la note de basse. Quatre cas sont présentés ci-dessous. Notez que dans le troisième cas, l'accord de *ré* est noté au-dessus de la portée et que dans le quatrième, le même accord est noté au milieu de la portée. Cela évite que les notes d'accord et de basse se retrouvent soit trop proches, soit trop éloignées.

Si la note de basse change mais que l'accord est répété, au lieu de noter l'accord à chaque fois, une barre oblique suivie du nom de la note de basse montre le changement de la note de basse sur le même accord.

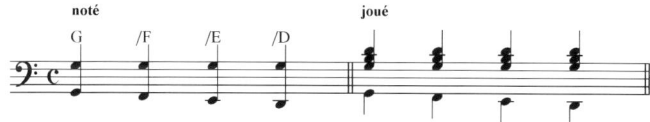

Pour les notes de basse et les accords, la notation utilisée est la notation internationale : B = *si*, F♯ = *fa* dièse, E♭ = *mi* bémol.

Annexe 2: Remarques sur les pièces

D-freygish Hora 2

Cette pièce en mode *freygish* est un parfait exemple du genre yiddish de la *hora*, en ternaire, avec son bel équilibre entre rythme et expression lyrique. Elle est placée en début de recueil car elle ne présente pas de difficulté technique et montre qu'une mélodie n'a pas besoin d'une harmonie complexe pour être profondément touchante. Comme la *hora* est une musique de danse, l'accompagnement devrait être régulier – mais non rigide.

Kandel's Hora 4

Autre exemple de *hora* yiddish ternaire, cette très belle mélodie a été enregistrée par de nombreux musiciens, dont le violoniste Max Leibowitz (sous le titre *Yiddish tants*). Les musiciens klezmer d'aujourd'hui l'appellent *Kandel's Hora*. Comme pour la *D-freygish Hora*, cet arrangement n'utilise que trois accords, pour ne pas distraire de l'expressivité de la mélodie.

Moldavian Yiddish Hora 6

Cette mélodie est parue sous le titre *Hora, n° 159*, dans un remarquable recueil de Petru Stoïanov intitulé *500 melodii de jocuri din Moldova* («500 airs de danse moldaves»), Chisinau : Cartea Moldoveneasca, 1972. Elle représente l'un des nombreux types différents de horas moldaves. Sans difficulté technique, elle demande cependant une grande subtilité dans l'émotion.

Moldavian Yiddish Suite 8

Cette suite rassemble trois joyeux airs de danse. Le premier est le *n° 182, zhok*, du recueil de Stoïanov (1972) (voir aussi *Moldavian Yiddish Hora*), le deuxième (à partir de B) est un air traditionnel intitulé *Jokul lui Tudoska* (Tudoska's zhok), et le troisième (à partir de C) est un *sher* traditionnel de Moldavie. Le tempo doit toujours être sautillant ; vous pouvez l'accélérer légèrement au début de chaque nouvelle pièce.

Dobridyen 14

Un *dobridyen* («bonjour») est un air joué pour accueillir les invités lors d'un mariage ou d'une autre occasion festive. La mélodie est très lyrique ; le tempo devrait être souple et riche en respirations, pour suivre le phrasé de la mélodie.

Nakhes fun kinder 16

Cet arrangement repose sur un enregistrement réalisé en Pologne au début du XXe siècle par un ensemble typique, le *Belf's Romanian Orchestra*. Le titre désigne le « sentiment d'être fier de ses enfants ». Malgré la simplicité de la mélodie, jouer la basse et les accords avec sentiment et en dialogue avec la mélodie n'a rien de facile. Le tempo devrait être régulier sans être rigide.

Gas nign 18

Un *gas nign* est une pièce que les *klezmorim* jouaient en marchant, pour accompagner un déplacement d'un lieu à un autre. Elle est d'un tempo et d'un caractère solennel, modéré. Cette pièce vous surprendra peut-être car elle sonne comme une sorte d'hybride de musique baroque et yiddish, changeant parfois d'une phrase à l'autre. L'arrangement exploite pleinement les harmonies impliquées par la mélodie, même si la pièce n'a probablement jamais été jouée ainsi par le passé. La basse et les accords devraient couler librement et ne pas entraver l'expressivité de la mélodie.

Khupe tants 20

Tirée d'un enregistrement d'Abe Schwartz datant du début du XXe siècle, *Khupe tants* («Danse de baldaquin de mariage»), cette pièce a de forts accents yiddish, qui la distinguent des autres musiques des Balkans ou d'Europe orientale. Les croches liées devraient être resserrées (voir l'*annexe 1: Ornementation et Phrasé*) et le rythme devrait « traîner » un peu, sans être trop lourd.

Sha, sha di shviger kumt 22

Le premier enregistrement de cette mélodie a été réalisé par le *Belf's Romanian Orchestra* en 1912 sous le titre *Dem Rebns Gavdule* («La Havdalah du rabbin»), mais l'enregistrement plus connu du clarinettiste Dave Tarras s'intitule *Sha, sha di shviger kumt* («Chut, chut, la belle-mère arrive»). Tarras (1897–1989), dont la carrière couvre presque tout le XXe siècle, a enregistré cette pièce au début du siècle, avant que les *bulgars* au tempo rapide ne deviennent populaires aux États-Unis au point d'évincer pratiquement tout le répertoire plus ancien. L'enregistrement de Tarras a été réédité de nombreuses fois au cours des vingt dernières années.

Dobranotsh 24

Un *dobranotsh* («bonne nuit») est un morceau qu'on joue à la fin d'un mariage ou d'une autre fête pour accompagner le départ des invités. Celui-ci est le septième air d'un recueil monumental, le *Jewish Instrumental Folk Music* de Moshe Beregovski, paru en 1937 et réimprimé en 2001 par *Syracuse University Press*. Beregovski note cette pièce en 3/4 avec un tempo de 132 à la noire. Je préfère un tempo un peu plus lent, noté à 3/8. Cette pièce devrait être jouée avec beaucoup de douceur et fluidité, en laissant chanter et respirer l'harmonie et la mélodie. L'harmonie et l'accompagnement restent assez simples jusqu'à la mesure 48. Vous pouvez reprendre *da capo* et terminer à la mesure 48 ou continuer jusqu'à la fin de la pièce : ici, l'accompagnement écrit est plus complexe et plus moderne.

Bukusher Chusid 27
Natif de Roumanie puis installé à New York, Joseph Moskowitz (1879–1954) était un virtuose du cymbalum. Ses nombreux enregistrements figurent sur bon nombre de compilations de musique klezmer et ses mélodies restent très populaires auprès des musiciens klezmer contemporains. Cet arrangement pour accordéon, techniquement exigeant, demande un toucher très léger.

Terkishers 30
Le *terkisher* se distingue par un motif rythmique marqué, qui devrait offrir une base stable à la mélodie. Cette suite combine deux airs enregistrés par le grand clarinettiste klezmer Naftule Brandwein (1884–1963), airs qu'il intitulait *Ziser Bulgar* («Bulgar doux») et *Fufzehn yahr fon der heim awek* («Quinze ans loin de la maison»). Pour l'accordéoniste, le défi consiste à prendre de grandes libertés rythmiques et lyriques avec la mélodie sans bousculer l'accompagnement.

Odessa Bulgar 32
Issue du répertoire de Mishka Ziganoff (voir aussi *Koilen*), cette pièce est plus un arrangement qu'une transcription d'enregistrement. Elle repose sur l'interaction des accents de la mélodie et de l'accompagnement. Gardez un son léger, pour que les accents ne deviennent pas trop lourds. L'enregistrement de Ziganoff est disponible sur YouTube.

Koilen 34
Le grand accordéoniste klezmer Mishka Ziganoff (1889–1967) a enregistré de nombreuses pièces, et son style léger et rythmique reste un modèle de référence pour la plupart des accordéonistes klezmer d'aujourd'hui. Cette pièce est une transcription de son enregistrement de *Koilen*, chanson populaire yiddish, réalisé en 1919. Elle montre très bien comment Ziganoff apporte des variations légères, mais

importantes, à la mélodie et à l'accompagnement de manière à ce que chaque reprise de la mélodie garde tout son intérêt. Ces variations figurent sur la partition, pour ceux qui voudraient étudier de plus près le style unique de Ziganoff. Vous pouvez aussi écouter la pièce sur YouTube.

Note : vous pouvez écouter plusieurs pièces de ce recueil (*Moldavian Yiddish Hora, Moldavian Yiddish Suite, Sha, sha di shviger kumt* et *Terkishers*) sur le CD *Splendor*, du groupe *The Other Europeans*.

Weitere Titel für Akkordeon

- Arvo Pärt • Ukuaru valss (2) * • UE 37 165
- Jenö Takács • Von fernen Küsten (2) • UE 19 928
- Alfred Schnittke • Zwei kleine Stücke (4) • UE 31 131
- Luciano Berio • Sequenza XIII (5) • UE 30 377

WORLD MUSIC

- Diego Collatti • Tango Accordion (3) • UE 36 120
- Petar Ralchev • Balkan Accordion (3) • UE 36 121
- Alan Bern • Klezmer Accordion (3) • UE 36 122
- Tommaso Huber & Marinette Bonnert • Dances from
  Flanders & Wallonia für Akkordeon (3) • UE 36 123
- Martin Tourish • Celtic Accordion (3) • UE 36 125

- Christian Dawid & Alan Bern • Klezmer Duets
  für Klarinette und Akkordeon (3) • UE 36 969
- Deborah Strauss & Alan Bern • Klezmer Duets
  für Violine und Akkordeon (3) • UE 37 189
- Martin Tourish • Celtic Duets
  für Flöte und Akkordeon (2–3) • UE 38 035

* Schwierigkeitsgrad / Approximate gradings
(1)–(5) = Leicht – Fortgeschritten / Easy – Advanced   814/I 19